SUPER POWER
Americans Today

TITLE LIST

The Northern Colonies: The Quest for Freedom (1600–1700)

The Southern Colonies: The Quest for Prosperity (1600–1700)

The Original United States of America:
Americans Discover the Meaning of Independence (1770–1800)

Thomas Jefferson's America: The Louisiana Purchase (1800–1811)

The Expanding United States: The Rise of Nationalism (1812–1820)

A Proud and Isolated Nation: Americans Take a Stand in Texas (1820–1845)

From Sea to Shining Sea: Americans Move West (1846–1860)

Americans Divided: The Civil War (1860–1865)

What the Land Means to Americans: Alaska and Other Wilderness Areas (1865–1890)

Crossing the Seas: Americans Form an Empire (1890–1899)

A World Contender: Americans on the Global Stage (1900–1912)

Super Power: Americans Today

What Makes America America?

SUPER POWER
Americans Today

BY
ERIC SCHWARTZ

MASON CREST PUBLISHERS
PHILADELPHIA

Mason Crest Publishers Inc.
370 Reed Road
Broomall, Pennsylvania 19008
(866) MCP-BOOK (toll free)

First printing
1 2 3 4 5 6 7 8 9 10

Library of Congress Cataloging-in-Publication Data

Schwartz, Eric.
  Super power : Americans today / by Eric Schwartz.
      p. cm. — (How America became America)
  Includes bibliographical references and index.
  ISBN 1-59804-912-4 ISBN 1-59804-900-0 (series)
  1. United States—Foreign relations—20th century—Juvenile literature. 2. United States—Foreign relations—2001—Juvenile literature. I. Title. II. Series.
  E744.S4144 2005
  973.9—dc22
                                    2004026704

Design by Dianne Hodack.
Produced by Harding House Publishing Service, Inc.
Cover design by Dianne Hodack.
Printed in the Hashemite Kingdom of Jordan.

CONTENTS

Introduction   6

1. Entering the World Stage: World War I and Its Aftermath   9

2. The Great Depression   27

3. World War II   43

4. Two Super Powers Emerge: The Cold War Era   51

5. The Last Super Power Standing   67

6. America Today   81

Timeline   86

Further Reading   90

For More Information   91

Index   92

Biographies   94

Picture Credits   95

INTRODUCTION

by Dr. Jack Rakove

Today's America is not the same geographical shape as the first American colonies—and the concept of America has evolved as well over the years.

When the thirteen original states declared their independence from Great Britain, most Americans still lived within one or two hours modern driving time from the Atlantic coast. In other words, the Continental Congress that approved the Declaration of Independence on July 4, 1776, was continental in name only. Yet American leaders like George Washington, Benjamin Franklin, and Thomas Jefferson also believed that the new nation did have a continental destiny. They expected it to stretch at least as far west as the Mississippi River, and they imagined that it could extend even further. The framers of the Federal Constitution of 1787 provided that western territories would join the Union on equal terms with the original states. In 1803, President Jefferson brought that continental vision closer to reality by purchasing the vast Louisiana Territory from France. In the 1840s, negotiations with Britain and a war with Mexico brought the United States to the Pacific Ocean.

This expansion created great opportunities, but it also brought serious costs. As Americans surged westward, they created a new economy of family farms and large plantations. But between the Ohio River and the Gulf of Mexico, expansion also brought the continued growth of plantation slavery for millions of African Americans. Political struggle over the extension of slavery west of the Mississippi was one of the major causes of the Civil War that killed hundreds of thousands of

Americans in the 1860s but ended with the destruction of slavery. Creating opportunities for American farmers also meant displacing Native Americans from the lands their ancestors had occupied for centuries. The opening of the west encouraged massive immigration not only from Europe but also from Asia, as Chinese workers came to labor in the California Gold Rush and the building of the railroads.

By the end of the nineteenth century, Americans knew that their great age of territorial expansion was over. But immigration and the growth of modern industrial cities continued to change the American landscape. Now Americans moved back and forth across the continent in search of economic opportunities. African Americans left the South in massive numbers and settled in dense concentrations in the cities of the North. The United States remained a magnet for immigration, but new immigrants came increasingly from Mexico, Central America, and Asia.

Ever since the seventeenth century, expansion and migration across this vast landscape have shaped American history. These books are designed to explain how this process has worked. They tell the story of how modern America became the nation it is today.

One

ENTERING THE WORLD STAGE: WORLD WAR I AND ITS AFTERMATH

Today, the United States of America is the world's lone super power. The United States has the greatest *economic* strength, the most military might, and perhaps the most political clout of any nation. Throughout human history, many individuals, nations, and empires have arisen to lead, conquer, or control large portions of the world (or at least the portions of the world known to them at the time). Some of these empires, like the Roman Empire for example, ruled for hundreds of years, but perhaps no nation in human history has ever wielded the type of global influence the United States holds today. Yet, at less than 250 years old, the United States is still a relatively young nation. So how did it reach a position of such prominence and power in this short amount of time?

As upstart colonies bickering with "Mother England," young America may not have seemed destined for such world might. In fact, less than one hundred years after its birth, the United States was already embroiled in a bloody civil war that threatened to

Economic means relating to the goods and services produced by a country.

9

*If something is **preeminent**, it is highly distinguished and stands out from others of its kind.*

bring down the nation. Yet, within another hundred years, the country was one of the **preeminent** powers in the world. How did it all happen? America's rise to world power was a process born largely through war. Great conflicts of the twentieth century defined the United States and its role in the world. They shaped the still-young America and ultimately led to America's birth as a super power.

AMERICA'S FIRST GREAT TEST ABROAD: WORLD WAR I

World War I began in 1914, and for three years its trenches defined hell for millions of men. Soldiers fought, ate, and slept with the dead around them. On what was known as the Western Front, barbed wire, mines, and trenches cut a swath from the North Sea all the way to the Swiss border. On one side of this front, the soldiers of the Central Powers (Germany, Austria-Hungary, the Ottoman Empire, and Bulgaria) dug in. On the other side, soldiers of the Allied forces (the United Kingdom, France, Belgium, Serbia, Montenegro, the Russian Empire, and eventually other countries from around the world) drew their lines. Between these battle positions lay the area called "no man's land," where any sign of life could be subjected to blistering machine-gun fire. Periodically, soldiers attempted to take the other line, only to be forced back by gunfire or poison gas. More than one million men died in battles along the Western Front. Their deaths achieved very little. The gain or loss of inconsequential pieces of territory, sometimes mere feet of land, was all the first three years of the war accomplished.

World War I poster

The trenches

A Wonderful
Opportunity
For YOU

Ashore, On Leave.

United States Navy

Propaganda posters encouraged Americans to enlist.

It was America's 1917 entry into World War I that changed the balance between the opposing forces. While they were comparatively unseasoned, American soldiers provided reserves for the exhausted Allied forces. When the Germans launched a spring offensive in March 1918, they came within fifty miles (80.5 km) of Paris, but 27,500 Americans, fighting their first important battle, drove the Germans out of the area in June. Within a month, 270,000 Americans fought back a German advance between Reims and Soissons. The Germans put everything into another push toward Paris, but that offensive

12

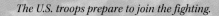

The U.S. troops prepare to join the fighting.

was defeated within three days, and the tide began to turn in the Allies' favor.

The Americans' impact grew as the numbers of soldiers increased. Between September 12 and 16, 500,000 American soldiers countered a German offensive at Saint-Mihiel. Two weeks later, 1.2 million American soldiers began the Meuse-Argonne offensive. After more than a month of bitter fighting, they broke through the Hindenberg Line. The British and French mounted a similar successful offensive, and on November 9, German Emperor Kaiser Wilhelm II ***abdicated***—a key demand of U.S. President Woodrow Wilson—and two days later, the German government accepted an ***armistice.***

On November 11, 1918, President Wilson announced the armistice to the U.S. Congress. As treaty negotiations began in

Abdicated *means to have resigned a position.*

*An **armistice** is a break in fighting to allow for peace negotiations.*

General Pershing

13

*If something is **humane**, it is compassionate and shows concern for life.*

*If something is **lenient**, it is not harsh and shows tolerance.*

***Reparations** are compensation for war demanded from the defeated party.*

While American and Allied troops fought mostly on the Western Front, World War I was also waged on the Eastern Front—the area along the Russian Empire's border stretching from the Baltic to the Black Sea.

Propaganda portrayed the Germans as inhuman monsters.

Europe, Wilson looked forward to the "great and hazardous tasks of political reconstruction." He wanted to use America's newly acquired clout to help negotiate a lasting peace and believed that such a peace could only be achieved if Europe agreed to a ***humane*** policy of reconstruction rather than revenge. Wilson stated, "Hunger does not breed reform; it breeds madness and all the ugly distempers that make an ordered life impossible."

Wilson's hopes for such a settlement got mired in the bitterness left by the long war. At Versailles, a suburb of Paris where most of the peace negotiations were hammered out behind closed doors, Wilson soon found himself outmaneuvered by the European diplomats. While he counseled for a ***lenient*** approach to the defeated Central Powers, the Allies declared Germany alone responsible for the war and demanded that it pay $33 billion in ***reparations***, a crushing sum for the war-torn nation. Germany also had to destroy tens of thousands of guns, locomotives, aircraft, and other military equipment. Its entire submarine fleet—the source of so much trouble for the Allies during the war—was

President Wilson reading the terms of the Armistice to Congress, November 11, 1918

SUPER POWER

Woodrow Wilson

eliminated, and most of its surface vessels were taken out of commission. The negotiation threatened to leave Germany a powerless, impoverished, and embittered nation—not an ideal recipe for lasting peace.

Nevertheless, President Wilson hoped that another result of the negotiations—the formation of an international body that could prevent wars in the future—would secure lasting peace. As part of the peace treaty, the League of Nations, a council of the world's major powers, would be formed. The hope was that countries could discuss and resolve grievances at the League of Nations before such disputes developed into a war like the one the world had just seen. Wilson wrote most of the charter for the organization. Article 10 of the *charter* was a *collective security agreement*, which called for members of the League to respect and preserve the territorial independence of the members.

After its role in the war, the United States had proven itself a nation to be reckoned with, but it would never become a member of the League. While President Wilson was in France, support for the Treaty of Versailles (as the agreement would be known) was eroding at home. Why? The United States, so newly born as a power on the world scene, did not want its affairs

*A **charter** is a statement of rights and responsibilities of an organization.*

*Countries that have a **collective security agreement** defend each other when attacked.*

Drawing representing the League of Nations' peaceful relationship

Edith Wilson: The "Secret President"

Edith Bolling was born in Virginia in 1872. Her childhood was privileged, happy, and full of social engagements. She married a businessman in 1896 and became well known in the Washington, D.C., area for her skills as a hostess. When her husband died unexpectedly, she learned keen business skills as well. In 1915, Edith married a widowed President Woodrow Wilson. Her skills as a hostess continued to shine, although entertaining at the White House was subdued because of the country's entry into World War I.

Edith's role in U.S. history changed when the President had a stroke in 1919. She was his constant companion and assumed many of his routine duties as the head of the government—all in secret and at the recommendation of his doctors. Edith decided what matters should be brought to the President's attention and directed all other matters to the appropriate department head. She did not make major decisions; she called her role one of "stewardship."

A **hemorrhage** is bleeding caused by a ruptured blood vessel.

Cynicism is expression of doubt or distrust of human nature or the sincerity of others.

The **status quo** is the way things are now.

dictated or governed by foreign powers or organizations (an attitude that continues to define the United States' relationship with the world today).

Wilson thought he could sway the U.S. Senate through public opinion, and in the fall of 1919, he launched a nationwide speaking tour, trying to rally support for the treaty. Shortly after a speech in Pueblo, Colorado, he suffered a brain **hemorrhage**. Unable to function as president for six weeks, Wilson's wife, Edith, took care of the routine presidential duties. Few, however, knew of Wilson's condition. For months afterward, Wilson was able to work only one hour a day, and he never fully recovered. While he got better physically, his judgment was affected by the brain trauma. This physical problem may have led to his obstinate stance on the League of Nations. While a compromise might have helped it through the U.S. Senate, Wilson refused to bend, and in 1920, the Treaty of Versailles fell short of the two-thirds needed for passage. The League of Nations became a reality for other nations, but the United States would not be part of President Wilson's brainchild.

AN ERA OF CYNICISM

The end of World War I was marked by a certain *cynicism*. The war had been described as a war to "make the world safe for democracy." Reality differed considerably from this ideal, and in the postwar period, democracy's safety at home and abroad was challenged.

Before World War I, the United States had experienced a strong Progressive movement, which pushed for social reforms like giving women the right to vote, outlawing child labor, protecting workers, and placing limitations on big business. Many Progressives, however, had been opposed to the war and persecuted by the government, which argued that opposition was

President and Mrs. Wilson

equal to treason. Progressives, however, weren't the only people persecuted in this period. Just about anything that might threaten the *status quo* could be perceived as dangerous.

The U.S. government used the general fears of the public to crush the Industrial Workers of the World (IWW), whose members were known popularly as the Wobblies and had a reputation as the most radical of the American unions. The Department of Justice raided forty-eight IWW meeting halls simultaneously in September 1917, collecting literature and letters. Within a

Agitators are people who try to arouse feelings and actions for a cause.

A *capitalist* country is one whose economic system is based on the private ownership of the means of production and distribution of goods is based on a free competitive market motivated by profit.

Bolsheviks were members of the Soviet party that eventually became the Communist Party.

Communists are those who support a classless society with the ownership and control of wealth and property given to the state.

In 1918, Socialist Party leader Eugene Debs was sentenced to ten years in prison for uttering these words: "The master class has always declared the wars; the subject class has always fought the battles. The master class has had all to gain and nothing to lose, while the subject class has had nothing to gain and all to lose—especially their lives."

Debs and the Socialist Party believed the "master class" was made up of wealthy individuals and businesses, which exploited the common worker (the subject class). They believed property and wealth should be held in common by all people rather than owned privately by individuals and businesses. In America, however, the right to private ownership is highly valued. Socialist ideas were far from popular, and Debs spent thirty-two months in prison for his beliefs. In 1921, he was released at the age of sixty-six. Today, most people would acknowledge that Debs' First Amendment right to free speech had been violated, but few would have argued on his behalf at the time lest they too be suspected of having socialist beliefs.

month, 165 IWW leaders were arrested for conspiracy to hinder the draft and other charges. More than one hundred IWW leaders were found guilty, and each was sentenced to up to ten years in prison and fined a total of $2,500,000. The union was essentially crushed.

In 1918, the government passed the Espionage Act, which made it a crime to interfere with the sale of war bonds or to use "abusive" language against the government, the

Leon Trotsky

Vladimir (Nicolai) Lenin

stalling governments of their own. These revolutionary movements, like that in the early United States, claimed to be of the people, by the people, and for the people, but the United States declared them to be global threats to democracy. Some people feared that labor unrest in the United States posed a similar threat.

Constitution, flag, or military uniforms. Violators were subject to fines or imprisonment. About two thousand people were prosecuted under the act, with nine hundred of them going to prison.

In postwar America, dissent was dangerous, especially during what came to be known as the Red Scare. In 1919 and 1920, the U.S. government aggressively persecuted social *agitators*. Why? Another world power was on the rise, and this one was nothing like the *capitalist* United States. In 1917, in the midst of World War I, the *Bolsheviks* had taken power in Russia. After the war, *communists* revolted in Hungary and Germany. In many areas of the world, poor people, long oppressed by governments that sucked the wealth of their nations, were agitating for change, even overthrowing their leaders and in-

Come On!

buy more LIBERTY BONDS

Political cartoons expressed outrage at Sacco's and Vancetti's executions.

People who are **anarchists** see no need for a formal system of government.

Mechanization is the process of changing a procedure so that a job previously done by a person is now done by a machine.

Something that is **nullified** has been made invalid.

U.S. Attorney General A. Mitchell Palmer pledged to aggressively counter any revolutionary movement. He hired J. Edgar Hoover to lead the Bureau of Investigation. (The Bureau of Investigation was combined with the Bureau of Prohibition in 1935 to form the Federal Bureau of Investigation [FBI].) Hoover's FBI spied on thousands of individuals and organizations. Palmer used this information to launch raids in thirty-three cities around the country, arresting about six thousand people. While Palmer said he hoped to catch revolutionary conspirators, no such conspiracy was uncovered, and most of the people arrested were never charged and soon released.

Probably the most famous "revolutionaries" arrested during the Red Scare were Nicola Sacco and Bartolomeo Vanzetti, two Italian immigrants and **anarchists**. They were charged with the murder of two people during a robbery at a shoe factory. Although there was clear evidence of misconduct by the judge and prosecution, a jury convicted them, and they were sentenced to death. Despite international protests, Sacco and Vanzetti were electrocuted on August 23, 1927.

The climate of fear and persecution was not limited to the government. It also permeated the general population with some terrible results. One striking example was the revival of the Ku Klux Klan (KKK), a white terrorist group that had thrived in the American South following the Civil War. In the 1920s, the KKK saw its membership rise to four million. During that decade, eight governors and about one dozen senators were elected because of strong backing by the KKK. The organization was also influential in convincing Congress to pass laws restricting new immigration.

Several factors were involved in the new drive to restrict immigration. The fear of communists abroad made some Americans fear foreigners in general. Another important factor was the *mechanization* of America's industry. In the past, industry needed lots of cheap labor, and industrialists had been some of immigration's strongest advocates. With this "progress," the need for manual labor decreased, and America's doors began closing.

Business played an important role in setting government policy during this decade. Congress lowered corporate taxes in 1921 and raised tariff rates the following year to protect domestic manufacturers. The government sold railroads, improved by taxpayer funds, back to private owners. Private owners also bought merchant ships built by the government. Many U.S. Supreme Court decisions weakened unions and protected business from government regulation. The Court *nullified* a law restricting child labor and overturned a minimum wage law for women.

A Ku Klux Klan float in a 1923 parade

ROARING DESPITE IT ALL

Despite the crackdown on just about anything that could be construed (or misconstrued) as communist or anti-capitalist in nature, culturally, the 1920s were a vibrant period in the United States. In fact, the decade is often called the "Roaring Twenties" for the fun-loving, rebellious side of the times. Movies, called motion pictures then, developed into a big business and an important American art form. In 1925, 60 million people attended movies every week, and by 1930 that figure had grown to 100 million, almost two times the number attending church weekly. The first

Fashions during the Roaring Twenties

23

Women Voters—At Last!

The 19th Amendment, which passed the Senate in 1919 and was ratified by the states in 1920, granted women the right to vote. After more than eighty years of struggle, the amendment became law when a majority of voters in two-thirds of the states approved the measure.

films were silent with separately recorded music scores and subtitles. Then, in 1927 Hollywood released *The Jazz Singer* starring Al Jolson. It was the first "talkie," and silent movies would soon be a thing of the past.

The 1920s are also sometimes called the "Jazz Age." Jazz originated in African American bars and gambling halls in the South. It also attracted rebellious, middle-class, white youth; and in the 1920s jazz spread north.

Radio helped popularize jazz, and this appliance became increasingly important in the twenties. Radio waves had been discovered in 1895, but several technological advances were required before commercial radio was established. In 1922, five hundred new radio stations sprang up. In 1926, the Radio Corporation of America (RCA) created the first national network of radio stations, the National Broadcasting Company (NBC).

Consumerism also exploded during the 1920s, and radio was partly responsible. Advertisers realized that radio could help them reach masses of people like never before, and they paid thousands of dollars to buy a minute of prime-time advertising. New products and appliances such as the phonograph, washing machine, sewing machine, and telephone became common in middle-class homes. As the use of electric appliances increased, so did the need for electricity. In 1912, 16 percent of the population lived in houses with electric lights. By 1927, almost four times as many homes had electricity.

Another important cultural influence was the automobile. Once far too expensive for the average family, cars suddenly became affordable through assembly-line mass production. Henry Ford led the way, producing the Model T at his modern factory complex in Detroit. By 1925, he was producing 9,000 cars a day. The high level of production allowed him to lower prices to $265, within reach of ordinary workers, who earned between $1,200 and $2,000 a year.

The automobile gave people (especially young people) greater independence and allowed them to move out of the inner cities. With quick, reliable transportation, people could live far from work. Inner-city populations decreased as suburbs were born. Rural areas also declined in population as more than 13 million Americans migrated from the countryside. America was on the move, but its path was still uncharted.

The Harlem Renaissance

African Americans moving to northern states sparked one of the great cultural phenomena of the twenties. Important African American writers including Langston Hughes and musicians such as Duke Ellington, Cab Calloway, and Bessie Smith adopted Harlem, a section of Manhattan, as their base, and an artistic and cultural movement sprang forth. The movement became known as the Harlem Renaissance, and Harlem became a vibrant and proud African American community, extending its influence far beyond New York City.

Guglielmo Marconi, radio inventor

Herbert Hoover

Two
THE GREAT DEPRESSION

In 1929, Herbert Hoover was inaugurated as president of the United States. In his inaugural address, Hoover declared that the United States had "reached a higher degree of comfort and security than ever before existed in the history of the world." That comfort and security would be deeply shaken before the year was over.

World War I and its immediate aftermath had been hard for Americans, but as the 1920s progressed, things seemed pretty good. Individual freedoms may have taken a hit, but America's businesses boomed. During the war, steel production and the *gross domestic product* (GDP) doubled. At the end of the war, the United States was the world's main economic power. U.S. trade accounted for roughly 30 percent of the world's commerce. New York displaced London as the banking center of the world, with U.S. financiers lending billions of dollars to businesses and governments around the globe.

A COMING CRASH

While so much was looking good, however, there were signs indicating trouble. Perhaps most worrisome was the huge differences in income levels. The combined income of the nation's 24,000 richest families was three times the combined income of the nation's

*The **gross domestic product** is the total value of all the goods and services produced in a country.*

*To be **conspicuous** is to be obvious, showy.*

*A business's **inventories** are the goods it has in stock and available for sale.*

__Interest rates__ are the fees people pay for borrowing money. For example, if you borrow money at a 10 percent interest rate, then every year that you don't pay the loan back, the amount of money you owe will grow by 10 percent.

__Speculation__ means engaging in risky transactions that are potentially profitable.

six million poorest families. The wealthiest one percent of the population saw their income increase by 75 percent, which represented nine percent of the total wage increases. But while millionaires indulged in ***conspicuous*** consumption, 40 percent of American households struggled to survive on incomes under $1,500 a year. As the nation's economy was based increasingly on consumerism, the fact that most people did not have enough money to live on was a serious problem. Since demand continued to increase, however, mass consumer credit was established, which allowed individuals to pay off purchases over time. By 1929, consumer debt had reached $7 billion, twice the size of the federal budget.

Like individuals, many corporations were in debt. To pay their bills, corporations began offering stock to the public. Buying stock was buying a tiny piece of a company—the stockholders became the company owners. The corporation could use the money from stocks to pay off debts. The stock market, however, had little regulation. Over the next decade, the concept of buying stocks "on margin" developed. This meant that individual investors bought stocks on credit, with little or no down payment. Investing in stocks was incredibly risky; if the company did well, then the stockholders made money; but if the company failed, the stockholders lost the money they had invested. Small and large investors were essentially gambling on Wall Street, buying millions of dollars of stock shares on margin. The stock market grew from $43 billion in 1925 to $64 billion in 1929.

With increased spending, rising debt, and unsound investment practices, something had to give. The first signs of economic decline appeared in the summer of 1929 when housing purchases dropped, consumer spending decreased, and business *inventories* increased. The Federal Reserve, the central bank of the United States, which oversees credit, *interest rates*, and money supply, tried to slow *speculation* on Wall Street by increasing interest rates. The higher interest rates didn't significantly affect that problem, but they did increase costs for consumers, further dampening demand.

The stock market continued to climb, with share prices setting new records in September. On October 21 and 22, the market showed gains, but for some reason on Wednesday morning, October 23, 1929, millions of shares were offered for sale on the New York Stock Exchange. When prices started to fall and just kept falling the next day, panic began. Stock prices seemed to be in a free fall as individuals rushed to sell their shares. By the end of the day, the market had lost $9 billion in value.

The banking and financial systems both operated with far less regulation than they do today, so when the economy began to collapse, there were almost no safeguards in place to restore stability. The problem with selling stocks is that if no one is willing to buy your share, you

Crowds mill around the New York Stock Exchange on October 24, 1929.

can't recover your investment. If there's no buyer, your share becomes worthless, and in late October 1929, no one was willing to buy into the crashing market. On October 29, "Black Tuesday," the stock market collapsed. More than 16 million shares were put up for sale at ever-lower prices. By the end of the month, more than $15 billion in stock value had been lost. By the end of the year, that loss had climbed to $40 billion, or about 60 percent of the total value of stocks listed on the Stock Exchange when the crash began.

Despite the seriousness of the stock market crash, few people fully grasped the impact that would ripple through the American and world economies. The ruined investors, lost fortunes, and even suicides were just the beginning. Next, consumer demand dried up. Companies could not sell their products and had to close their factories. An average of 100,000 workers lost their jobs every week that year. Two million were unemployed by the end of 1929. That number grew to four million in 1930, and by 1932 reached 12 million people. The economic downturn this started would be known as the Great Depression, which defined the decade of the 1930s and profoundly shaped American society for years to come.

The economic situation improved slightly in the spring of 1931, and President Hoover even declared the economic depression over. But in July, the American economy again declined as European economies collapsed. American consumers weren't buying much of anything—European or American. Many European governments were forced to **default** on debts. National currencies became unstable. Even Great Britain was forced to take the pound, its currency, off the **gold standard**. It became painfully clear how linked all the major economies of the world

had become. Hoover blamed the United States' continuing economic problems on Europe, but in fact, the European problems were caused by the United States.

During the last years of the Hoover administration, the Great Depression worsened. By the fall of 1931, unemployment reached eight million, or about 18 percent of the workforce, and unrest was stirring. In May 1932, unemployed World War I veterans organized a march on Washington, asking Congress to pay their insurance bonus early. The bonus wasn't due until 1945, but money was needed to pay debts and feed families. Congress refused to budge. Most of the veterans returned home, but about 2,000 of them, some with their families, stayed in the capital, setting up a camp and occupying vacant public buildings. Although they were not a serious threat to public safety, President Hoover ordered the police to kick the veterans out of public buildings. Violence erupted at one site, several policemen were injured, and Hoover ordered the U.S. Army to chase all of the veterans out of Washington. The army used cavalry, infantry, tear gas, machine guns, and tanks to attack the "Bonus Marchers." They gassed the veterans; burned their huts; and chased unarmed men, women, and children with tanks.

Julius Rosenwald, president of the Sears, Roebuck and Company, after the stock market crash

Another example of the upheaval job loss created was seen at the Ford River Rouge Plant. By 1932, three-quarters of the employees had lost their jobs. When unemployed workers marched to the gates of the plant to ask for jobs, guards shot at the men, killing four and wounding many others.

It was an election year, and events like the rout of the Bonus Marchers and the killings at River Rouge weren't good publicity for President Hoover, whose policies in general seemed to have failed the country. The Democratic candidate, Franklin Delano Roosevelt, then governor of New York, pledged a "New Deal for the

*Governments who **default** on loans do not pay them back.*

*The **gold standard** is a system of defining monetary units in terms of their value in gold.*

A "rush" on a bank after the stock market crash

From Breadbasket to Dust Bowl

Beginning in 1931, severe drought in the Midwest and southern plains deepened the Great Depression. Farmland turned to dust. Crops shriveled, animals died, and windstorms blew away the impoverished topsoil. The Breadbasket of America was now the nation's Dust Bowl.

The government passed legislation, like buying cattle and opening federal lands to grazing, to help the farmers and ranchers. This legislation brought some small relief, but it could not bring rain. The drought and dust storms grew to eventually cover twenty-seven states. Many farm families were forced to move to the cities to find work, which was already in short supply. They were not always welcomed. In February 1936, Los Angeles police set up patrols at the Arizona and Oregon borders to keep out the "undesirables."

In the fall of 1939, Mother Nature did what the government could not. Rain began to fall, and the drought was finally over.

Franklin Delano Roosevelt

American people" and promised to help the "forgotten man" in dire economic straits. On Election Day, Roosevelt received almost 23 million votes to Hoover's 15.8 million. The Democrats also gained the largest majorities in both houses of Congress since before the Civil War. It was the most dramatic political reversal in American history.

A NEW LEADER AND A "NEW DEAL"

Roosevelt may have won the election, but before his inauguration on March 4, 1933, the toll of the Depression deepened. That winter proved to be the worst of the Depression. More than 13 million people were unemployed. Thousands of individuals and businesses went bankrupt. One day before Roosevelt's inauguration, thirty-eight states closed all their banks; in the remaining states, preparations for closings were under way. The New York Stock Exchange suspended trading because there were simply no buyers to be found.

Democratic candidate Franklin Delano Roosevelt

On March 4, Roosevelt fought the mood of desolation with one of his most powerful weapons: words. In his inaugural address Roosevelt declared, "The only thing we have to fear is fear itself—nameless, unreasoning, unjustified terror." Roosevelt promised bold moves to shake the country out of the Great Depression. That night, rather than attending an inaugural ball, Roosevelt gathered financial experts together to devise a plan for the country. The following day, he declared a "bank holiday," giving bank examiners time to determine which banks could be reopened safely. He also called Congress, which was recessed, back into emergency session to deal with the situation.

The next three months became known as "The Hundred Days." During this time, Roosevelt's administration drafted and Congress passed numerous bills meant to aid a struggling America. The Civilian Conservation Corps, for example, was created to employ the hundreds of thousands of Americans who were out of work. In the next ten years, the program employed more than 2 million young men in

A New Kind of First Lady

Eleanor Roosevelt

Eleanor Roosevelt redefined the role of First Lady, who previously had been seen as no more than the President's wife. When Franklin Roosevelt was governor of New York, Eleanor became his eyes and ears to what was going on in the "real" world. She continued this role throughout his life. As First Lady, she traveled extensively on fact-finding missions for the President, gave press conferences and radio addresses, and wrote a daily newspaper column. She served as a tireless advocate for the disadvantaged, and became involved in civil rights projects.

Eleanor Roosevelt's involvement in human rights did not end with her husband's death. In 1945 she became the American spokesperson in the United Nations, becoming the chairperson of the UN Human Rights Commission in 1946. President John F. Kennedy appointed her head of the Commission on the Status of Women in 1961. The former First Lady stated, "When you cease to make a contribution, you begin to die."

tasks such as building bridges and campsites. A less popular bill was the Agricultural Adjustment Act, designed to increase farmers' income. The Agriculture Department ordered millions of acres of farmland to be withdrawn from cultivation. The idea was to decrease the supply of food in order to boost prices. Though this caused an uproar because millions of Americans were going hungry, farm income rose for the first time since World War I.

Another major reform was the National Industrial Recovery Act (NIRA). The act created the National Recovery Administration (NRA), which set minimum wages and maximum work hours. NIRA also created the Public Works Administration, which allocated $3.3 billion for public works projects such as the construction of roads and public buildings. The New Deal also included legislation to address the problem of stock market speculation and created the Federal Deposit Insurance Corporation to make sure that individuals' bank accounts would be safe.

The New Deal proved to be popular with the public, but it had critics too. Businesspeople complained about excessive government interference and taxation. Other critics charged that New Deal programs offered insufficient relief to the American people. Others said the industrial policy programs often helped big businesses more than workers or small businesses. But the New Deal's most effective critics were in the Supreme Court. On May 27, 1935, the Court struck down important parts of the New Deal. They

National Recovery Administration poster

Huey Long

Huey Long

Huey Long was a strong critic of President Roosevelt's New Deal. A former governor of Louisiana, Long was elected to the U.S. Senate in 1932. In 1934, he created the Share Our Wealth Society and proposed seizing all incomes over one million dollars and all estates of five million dollars or more. With these funds, Long proposed to offer each family $5,000 for buying a farm or home, an annual income of $2,000, and other benefits. The program was not financially possible, and the Senate rejected Long's tax measures. But Long's political popularity continued to grow, and he planned to challenge Roosevelt in the 1936 election. In 1935, however, Huey Long was assassinated by the son-in-law of a political opponent.

Fireside Chats

President Franklin Roosevelt became famous for his "fireside chats," informal radio addresses to the American people. Known for their comforting but not condescending tone, the chats addressed topics ranging from bank failure to war. The first was broadcast on March 12, 1933. Between one-quarter and one-third of the workforce was unemployed, and every bank in America had been closed for the previous eight days. Roosevelt's chat explained how the problem had developed and what would be done about it. He explained the banking system in clear terms and announced that the banks would open the next day with deposits insured by the federal government. Roosevelt gave thirty broadcasts over the next twelve years. The format was a revolutionary change for a president because of their informal and direct approach, a form of communication that no president since Roosevelt has mastered so successfully.

ruled that the NRA, for example, was unconstitutional because it *ceded* too much power to the President.

Critics didn't deter Roosevelt. Before the Supreme Court even issued its opinion, the Roosevelt administration submitted legislation to create a second New Deal. The new legislation was, if anything, more progressive than the first, and its effects can still be seen. The Emergency Relief Appropriation Act (ERAA), for example, put millions of unemployed Americans to work. It funded the Works Progress Administration (WPA), which employed approximately 8.5 million people over the next eight years. More than 1 million projects, including thousands of buildings, roads, and bridges, were completed, and the WPA even employed writers, painters, and musicians. The Rural Electrification Administration subsidized construction of power lines to bring power into rural areas. In 1935, fewer than 10 percent of rural homes had electricity; by 1950, 90 percent did. The National Labor Relations Act strengthened workers' right to organize, creating the National Labor Relations Board to oversee votes on unionization. The board also had the power to sanction companies that treated workers unfairly.

*If something is **ceded** it is given away.*

Perhaps the most important New Deal program was the Social Security Act, signed in 1935, which established a partial pension plan for the elderly. The program also provided for people with disabilities, the unemployed, and mothers with dependent children. While it was not as generous as some European social insurance programs, the act was significant because it was official recognition of the government's responsibility to care for its citizens.

STORM CLOUDS

While the United States appeared to be making progress in addressing its problems at home, storm clouds were gathering on foreign horizons. Perhaps most ominously, Adolph Hitler was appointed chancellor of Germany in 1933. Germany was still struggling with the effects of World War I, and the insecure nation was looking for a strong leader who could restore Germany's position in the world. Hitler's Nationalist Socialist Workers (Nazi) Party exerted a powerful appeal with a German people weary of chaos and humiliation. Hitler promised to restore Germany's lost honor, ex-

Hitler and the Nazi flag

*In Nazi terms, to be **Aryan** was to be a Caucasian person of non-Semitic descent.*

*To **consolidate** is to combine separate items into a single one.*

The sign reads: "Germans, defend your-selves, do not buy from Jews."

The Holocaust

Hitler's attempt to exterminate the Jewish people is called the Holocaust. About nine million Jewish people lived in Europe in 1933. By the war's end, two out of three Jews in Europe had been killed in concentration and extermination camps. The Nazis also persecuted Roma (Gypsies), people with disabilities, homosexuals, Polish people, political dissidents, and minority religious groups.

By the 1930s, the Nazis' policy of persecution of the Jewish people was well known, and by 1942 the governments of the United States and Great Britain had confirmed reports of the "Final Solution." In 1943, Jan Karski, a leader of the Polish Resistance, personally met with President Roosevelt and described the genocide he had seen firsthand. Karski proposed that the concentration and extermination camps used by the Nazis be attacked. But only limited attempts were made to stop them, and neither the United States nor Great Britain modified its refugee process to help those fleeing the Nazis' campaign of death.

alting the ideal of an "***Aryan*** race," which supposedly represented the core of Germany. According to Hitler, internal enemies such as Jewish people and communists, were to blame for all of Germany's problems.

Soon after his appointment, Hitler began to **consolidate** political control. His brown-shirted party militia stirred up local violence and used the resulting chaos as an excuse to take over the provincial governments. In times of chaos, the Nazi's claimed, people needed someone strong to protect them, and Hitler and his party intended to be this "protector." The burning of the Reischstag, the German parliament building, on February 27, 1933, was used as an excuse to suspend civil liberties as police arrested communist leaders and political activists. By the elections of March 1933, the Nazis could confidently announce that these would be the "last elections for a hundred years."

The elections gave the Nazis and their allies a majority in Germany's parliament, clearing the way for Hitler to tighten his grip on the country. The Communist and Socialist parties were banned. On June 30, 1934, elite Nazi squads murdered at least one hundred political leaders, many of them former allies of the Nazis. After the President of Germany died on August 2, 1934, the cabinet approved Hitler's proposal to combine the offices of president and chancellor. Hitler's rise to power in Germany was now complete, and he was already looking beyond his country's borders.

Germany was not the only trouble spot in the world, and Americans were not oblivious to events beyond their shores. Nevertheless, the United States was wary of becoming involved in international conflicts. One of these conflicts occurred in 1935 when Italy prepared to invade Ethiopia. The following year, conflict erupted in

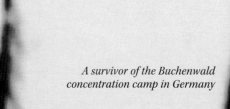

A survivor of the Buchenwald concentration camp in Germany

*A **fascist** is someone who supported a government characterized by a dictatorship, central control of private enterprise, repression of all opposition, and extreme nationalism.*

*A **Republican** government is one where the people elect representatives to exercise power for them.*

*A **satellite** is a country dependent on another country.*

Francisco Franco

Spain when Francisco Franco, a **fascist** army officer, led Spanish army units revolting against Spain's elected government. A brutal civil war ensued, and while most Americans remained neutral in the conflict, there was notable sympathy for the **Republican** government. A group of Americans even formed the Abraham Lincoln Battalion, which went to Spain to fight on the side of the anti-fascists.

Hitler watched the aggressions of other fascist governments approvingly, and soon he began his own program of territorial expansion. In 1938, he annexed Austria, the country of his birth. There was no meaningful objection by any country. By the fall, Hitler was demanding that Czechoslovakia give Germany a border region inhabited by many ethnic Germans. Czechoslovakia, the only democracy in Eastern Europe, prepared its army and sought assistance from other European countries. The Soviet Union and France had a treaty to assist the Czechs, but they refused to honor it. Abandoned by their allies, the Czechs had little choice but to surrender the territory. European leaders gathered in Munich to work out the details of the agreement, which the Prime Minister of England, Neville Chamberlain, proclaimed would ensure "peace for our time." In fact, the peace lasted little more than six months, after which German troops marched in and took the rest of Czechoslovakia.

Across the Pacific from the United States, Japan had steadily been increasing its military strength and territory. In 1931, the Japanese army had invaded Chinese Manchuria, but no nation was in a position to stop the Japanese aggression. In 1937, Japan continued its aggression by invading northern China. Japanese soldiers committed numerous atrocities, including the killing of thousands of civilians and the bombing of Chinese cities. The United States sold military arms and equipment to China, but fearing war with Japan, stopped short of imposing economic sanctions on that country.

Back in Europe, Hitler was heating things up. At the beginning of 1939, Hitler had offered the Poles status as a *satellite* country, viewing them as a potential ally in the war he was planning against the Soviet Union. When the Polish government rejected his offer, Hitler decided the country must be destroyed. In September 1939, World War II officially began with the German invasion of Poland. The Polish army resisted bravely but futilely. Its forces were hopelessly outgunned by German troops, and German tanks just rolled onto the flat plains of Poland.

The British and French governments were now wary of Hitler's growing power. They had previously signed security pacts with both Poland and Romania. In contrast to their response to Hitler's invasion of Czechoslovakia, the English and French stayed true to their defense treaties and declared war on Germany. This did not affect the fate of Polish troops, however. Within a month, the Nazis and the Soviet army had overrun Poland.

Hitler announcing Germany's acquisition of Austria

The crematoriums in a German concentration camp, where the bodies of countless Jews were burned

World War II poster

Three
WORLD WAR II

WAR ABROAD BUT "NEUTRAL" AT HOME

For the first eighteen months of World War II, the Germans were invincible. In April 1940, Hitler introduced the world to the concept of *blitzkrieg*, or lightning war. Within a month, the Germans conquered Denmark, Norway, the Netherlands, Luxembourg, and Belgium. The French felt secure behind their Maginot Line, a defensive perimeter built during World War I, but the Germans simply went around it, and the French army was practically defeated within two weeks. Paris fell on June 16. The Germans occupied the north of the country and set up a government of collaborators in the south.

The British finally understood the gravity of the situation. Following the fall of France, they evacuated 330,000 British soldiers from the north of France, abandoning weapons and equipment but saving the army. Neville Chamberlain, who had championed the Munich Agreement as a promise of "peace for our time," resigned in May 1940 and was replaced by a combative Winston Churchill. The Battle of Britain, an air war, raged in the British skies all summer.

In the United States that summer, Congress dedicated $8 billion to building up the country's military. It was the largest sum ever allocated for the military during peacetime. The boost in military spending gave the nation a final push out of the Depression as factories strived to fulfill new military orders. By the end

The U.S.S. Arizona *burning after the Japanese attack on Pearl Harbor*

of 1940, U.S. plants manufactured thousands of planes, pieces of heavy artillery, and tanks. Congress also began the first peacetime draft of soldiers.

Despite boosting its military and giving aid to the Allies, the United States would not declare war on Germany. President Roosevelt, who that year was elected to an unprecedented third term, also attempted to keep the United States out of the conflicts raging in Asia. Japan could not be swayed from its expansionist policy as it marched across the countries of Southeast Asia. Finally, in the summer of 1941, the United States embargoed all oil and steel shipments, materials needed for their war effort, to Japan. The two sides continued to talk, but neither side was willing to make concessions. In Europe at the same time, Germany invaded the Soviet Union, despite a nonaggression agreement, and appeared to be unstoppable as they rolled over the Soviet army.

As the end of 1941 drew near, conflict boiled all over the world, and it looked like the United States could not remain neutral. In fact, the U.S. military had already broken the main code used by Japanese diplomats to send messages. One intercepted message referred to a November 26 deadline for reaching an agreement with the United States. On November 27, Washington sent an alert to all U.S. military commanders in the Pacific warning them to expect "an aggressive move by Japan" within the next few days.

A SURPRISE ATTACK

For George Phraner, an Aviation Machinist's Mate on the U.S.S. *Arizona*, December 7, 1941, started out as a relaxed Sunday morning. The first indication of trouble came when a strange noise disturbed the usual morning quiet. Phraner and his shipmates left their breakfast to investigate. They saw airplanes over nearby Ford Island. Plumes of smoke were rising from the area, but the men didn't completely understand until they saw the Rising Sun emblem on the airplanes. These were Japanese planes, and the bombing of Pearl Harbor had begun.

The gun crews had practiced defensive actions countless times, but now they discovered that the guns on deck had only limited ammunition. Phraner was ordered to go deep into the ship to bring back more. While he was below, the Japanese hit a gunpowder storage area. One and a half million pounds of gunpowder exploded, ripping the ship apart and killing the rest of the gun crew.

Phraner somehow struggled through the blinding smoke and jumped off the ship before it sank. He swam to shore, and after a week recovering was transferred to the U.S.S. *Lexington*, which was sailing to engage the Japanese in the Coral Sea.

Many people had expected an act of sabotage, not a military attack by the Japanese. What happened at Pearl Harbor shocked

St. Paul's Cathedral in London amid the destruction of the Battle of Britain

America. The forces in Hawaii were taken by complete surprise—their fleet was destroyed and more than 2,400 soldiers were killed. On the same day, the Japanese attacked U.S. military bases in Guam and on Midway Island, and U.S. airplanes based in the Philippines were destroyed. The time for neutrality was clearly over. On December 8, President Roosevelt asked Congress to declare war on Japan. Three days later, Japan's allies, Germany and Italy, declared war on the United States.

Rationed tires

ENTERING THE FRAY

The Japanese followed these attacks by seizing Hong Kong, Java, and the Philippines. The tide began to turn, however, when the U.S. Navy won the Battle of the Coral Sea in May. One month later, the United States destroyed four Japanese aircraft carriers in the Battle of Midway, which prevented the Japanese from gaining a further foothold on the islands of the Pacific.

Late in 1942, battles came to new shores as British and U.S. forces landed in North Africa under the command of General Dwight Eisenhower. While the Americans had sought an invasion of Europe, the British thought the Germans would be weaker around the edges of their territory.

The battles in North Africa provided the American troops with their first real combat experience. General George S. Patton Jr., who later played a key role in Europe, served as field commander during the North African campaign, and Eisenhower gained both stature and valuable experience as the Allies defeated one of Hitler's best generals, Field Marshall Erwin Rommel, the "Desert Fox."

More good news came in 1943 when, after losing 300,000 men, the Germans surrendered at the Battle of Stalingrad in southern Russia. The Allies were also inflicting losses on the Germans at sea and from the air. Many of the dreaded German submarines were destroyed. This opened up the Atlantic Ocean to the shipping of military supplies. By the end of the year, Allied planes were heavily bombing German cities and military installations.

THE HOME FRONT

At home, the United States was firmly on a war footing. A new government agency controlled prices and rationed goods such as sugar, butter, gasoline, and coffee. Other controls, such as a ban on "pleasure driving" and a 35-mile-per-hour speed limit, were imposed to conserve fuel.

Food and fuel weren't the only things in short supply. The draft and the increased production of military equipment created a shortage of labor as well. In response, the government mounted a *propaganda* campaign encouraging women to take jobs out of the house. The female labor force increased from 25 to 36 percent, and "Rosie the Riveter" became a popular *icon*. She symbolized women's strength and ability to perform jobs like welding and operating machinery, jobs previously performed only by men. Between 1941 and 1945, more than six million women entered the U.S. labor force, about half of them in the manufacturing sector.

THE TIDE TURNS

Despite progress in Africa, it was clear that the Allies needed to defeat Germany in Europe if they were to win the war. By the spring of 1944, the Allies were planning an invasion. That invasion came on June 6—D-Day. On that fateful day, 150,000 American, French, British, Canadian, and Polish soldiers landed on the coast of Normandy, France. Storming the beaches as bullets rained from the cliffs was nearly suicidal, but the soldiers were determined to take the coast. Many drowned in the turbulent waters. Many

Propaganda is information distributed by an organization or government to spread and promote a policy, idea, or cause.

To be an *icon* is to be a symbol.

"We'll have lots to eat this winter, won't we Mother?"

**Grow your own
Can your own**

World War II poster encouraging Americans to grow their own food

The American Concentration Camps

An American concentration camp for Japanese Americans

During World War II, the United States had its own concentration camps called internment camps. After the bombing of Pearl Harbor, 120,313 Japanese Americans living in the states of California, Oregon, Washington, and Arizona had their homes, businesses, and properties seized and were imprisoned. Officials said the internment was to protect Americans from sabotage and espionage, but really it was a campaign of racism. Approximately 41,000 of the prisoners were first-generation immigrants, and approximately 72,000 were second-generation American citizens. The camps, most of which were built on American Indian reservations, operated from May 1942 until December 1947. Many of those interred never recovered—emotionally or financially—from the ordeal.

The American government also targeted Italian Americans for discriminatory treatment. About 1,200 Italians, including about 300 American citizens, were put in detention centers until Italy surrendered to the Allies in 1943. About 700,000 other Italian Americans faced special controls, such as travel restrictions and confiscation of cameras. More than 10,000 Germans were also detained at camps or military bases from 1941 to 1945.

others fell as they scrambled up the beach. Approximately 10,000 Allied troops were killed, but the Germans could not overcome the waves of soldiers breaking against the shore. The Allies successfully seized the beaches, and by July 26, they had broken through the German lines and were marching across France. They liberated Paris on August 25.

The Germans' final counteroffensive was in December 1944, when they pushed through Allied lines in Belgium. This thrust, however, was fought back, and by the spring of 1945 the Nazi regime was collapsing. The U.S. army reached the Rhine River, the traditional border of Germany, by the spring. The Soviet army took Berlin in April. American forces under Eisenhower defeated the remaining opposition, and Germany formally surrendered on May 7, 1945.

Throughout 1944, the Americans had also inflicted defeats on their Japanese foes. More than 273 Japanese fighter planes were destroyed in the Battle of the Philippine Sea in June 1944. By November, American pilots were conducting devastating raids on Japanese cities, killing hundreds of thousands of civilians in the final six months of the war. The Japanese, however, continued to fight fiercely despite their losses. In the spring of 1945, bitter battles were fought on Iwo Jima and Okinawa. By the time Okinawa was captured on June 22, the Japanese had inflicted more than 50,000 casualties on the Americans in three months of fighting.

Many feared the bloody battle with Japan would drag on indefinitely, but a new weapon was about to change warfare and the world forever. In July, the first atomic bomb was tested in the sands of New Mexico. Harry S. Truman, who became president when Roosevelt died of a brain hemorrhage, ordered that the weapon be used against Japan as soon as it was ready. Truman gave Japan one warning: it faced "utter devastation of the Japanese homeland" if it did not surrender unconditionally. The ultimatum was ignored.

At the end of July, Truman ordered the plan into action. At 8:45 A.M. on August 6, a U.S. bomber, the *Enola Gay*, dropped the atom bomb on Hiroshima, Japan. More than 80,000 people were killed immediately, turned to cinders by the heat of the bomb. Still, the Japanese did not surrender. On August 8, a second atom bomb was dropped, this time on Nagasaki. It was almost twice as powerful as the first but killed fewer people—45,000—because it missed its primary target.

Though Japanese military leaders were prepared to go on fighting, the Japanese Emperor personally persuaded them to surrender. With that, World War II was over. More than 17 million soldiers and 37 million civilians were dead.

Atomic bomb test

Four
TWO SUPER POWERS EMERGE: THE COLD WAR ERA

For centuries, Western European powers dominated the world. They ruled over colonies in Asia, Africa, and the Americas, creating vast empires that stretched across the earth. But the World Wars had all but crushed the Western European empires, and two countries were more than willing to step into the power vacuum and seize their place as global leaders. The United States and the Soviet Union would dominate world affairs for decades to come.

The capitalist United States and the communist Soviet Union had been reluctant allies during World War II. Before the war began, each had been suspicious of the other's government and politics, and their relationship remained strained. Each suspected the other of desiring world domination, and the Soviet Union seemed to display this desire when it marched across Eastern Europe, liberating those countries from Nazi control, setting up communist governments in their place.

In their struggle for supremacy, the United States and Soviet Union entered a race to develop a nuclear weapon. The United States won that race; Hiroshima and Nagasaki proved that no one could argue with the wielder of "The Bomb." The Soviet Union, however, wasn't going to stand by while the United States became the

Ideologically *means based on a specific belief system.*

Intelligence networks *are organizations, usually highly secretive, that gather information about other countries, organizations, or people.*

Subjugation *is the act of bringing a person, group, or country under the control of another, often by military conquest.*

sole power of the world. They soon had a nuclear bomb of their own. Two completely **ideologically** opposed governments now had the power to annihilate each other—and the world. No one knew how to handle such colossal power, and the two countries entered a period of hostility called the Cold War. To many people, it seemed that existence itself hung in the balance.

With neither side willing to fire a shot and risk nuclear war, the United States and Soviet Union looked for other ways to dominate each other. This meant amassing allies, supporting sympathetic governments, establishing **intelligence networks**, and placing weapons wherever possible in the world. Both countries looked for ways to promote their own forms of governments and economies around the world.

A Life of Fear

Fallout shelter symbol

During the second half of the twentieth century, the cryptic yellow and black sign was evident on just about any public school. It indicated the presence of a bomb shelter, almost always in a basement or sub-basement, where people could take refuge in the event of a nuclear attack. The bomb shelters and the "duck-and-cover" drills in which children hid under their desks were accepted responses to the threat of nuclear annihilation that hung over the world during the Cold War. You can still see these signs hanging in many public places.

The Truman Doctrine is a good example of how the Cold War affected international relations. In 1947, President Harry S. Truman committed the United States to "support free peoples who are resisting attempted *subjugation* by armed minorities or by outside pressures." The new policy essentially divided the world between "free countries" and areas of "terror and oppression." It also regarded all communists as dangerous, a policy that would have huge repercussions. When the United States suspected communists were becoming too powerful in Turkey and Greece, for example, it gave $400 million in military assistance to the two countries.

To help stem communist advances, the Truman administration also proposed the European Recovery Program, widely known as the Marshall Plan after George C. Marshall, the secretary of state who unveiled it. Because communist philosophies were based on the idea that all people should share property and wealth, communism was much more popular in poverty-stricken areas than in economically stable areas. Western Europe was certainly poverty stricken after World War II, and the United States feared that economic hardship would

Korean civilians

make Western Europe a prime breeding ground for communism. By helping Western Europe rebuild, the United States hoped to thwart communism and instill capitalist democracy in the region. By 1950, the Marshall Plan had distributed $35 billion in U.S. aid to the countries of Western Europe, restoring that region's economy and stabilizing the area politically.

Truman signing the proclamation of a "national emergency," which was the basis for the Korean War

WAR IN CHINA AND KOREA

While Western Europe was rebuilding, other parts of the world were becoming increasingly unstable. China endured a civil war between the Communist Party of China and the Kuomintang (Nationalist Party). The nationalist forces, with considerable U.S. support, had captured the major cities in China, but the communists held the countryside, which contained more than 85 percent of the population. By the summer of 1949, the Nationalists were surrendering in large groups, and before the end of the year the President of the nationalists fled with his supporters to the island of Formosa (now called Taiwan).

U.S. political and military experts argued over "Who lost China?" Some Republicans blamed the Democratic-controlled Congress for not providing sufficient aid to the Nationalists, but in retrospect, analysts have concluded that the Nationalists were probably doomed to failure. The communists promised the peasants land reform and social equality. The

Nationalist forces were corrupt, inept, and made little attempt to appeal to the Chinese peasants, who formed the majority of the Chinese people.

Nonetheless, the critics were effective in persuading many American voters that the Truman administration had been too soft on the communists. Then, on June 25, 1950, communist North Korean forces invaded noncommunist South Korea. Not wanting to make the same mistake twice, President Truman immediately committed U.S. troops to defend South Korea. The United Nations (UN) Security Council endorsed the U.S. intervention, but the United States provided about 90 percent of the ground forces.

In August 1950, UN forces under General Douglas MacArthur pushed the North Koreans back to their country's original border. Truman, however, ordered forces to keep pushing the North Koreans back, changing the nature of the war from a defensive exercise to protect South Korea to an offensive war to liberate the North Koreans from their communist government. As the UN forces approached North Korea's border with China, the Chinese government warned it would intervene if the UN forces kept going. General MacArthur and the Truman adminis-

tration ignored these warnings, and more than 300,000 Chinese troops swarmed across the border at the end of November. The UN troops were pushed back down the Korean peninsula.

UN troops were able eventually to fight their way back to the original border. MacArthur, meanwhile, was arguing with Truman because he thought the conflict should be brought to China using whatever means necessary. Truman, however, feared a war that could grow uncontrollably and eventually pull the Soviet Union in on China's side. After MacArthur refused to back down, Truman dismissed the successful, but difficult, general.

On July 27, 1953, an armistice was reached, establishing borders that were essentially identical to those before the North Korean invasion. About 54,000 American and hundreds of thousands of Korean and Chinese soldiers died in the three-year conflict.

American soldiers in Korea

General MacArthur

LOST IN THE JUNGLE

While communism had taken hold in China and North Korea, a communist movement was also under way in Vietnam. Before World War II, France had controlled Vietnam and its neighbors. The Japanese then seized control, but as World War II drew to a close, the Vietnamese communist leader Ho Chi Minh saw an opportunity for his country to become independent. In 1945, his rev-

The McCarthy Era

Truman and the Democratic-controlled Congress were criticized for being soft on communism. In 1952, Dwight D. Eisenhower and the Republican Party swept the elections, taking the presidency and both congressional houses. Some of the conservative Republicans used their newfound power to seek out and destroy "communist threats" in the United States. The most notorious was Senator Joseph McCarthy, who had already begun a campaign against supposed communists in the government. Now his crusade gained strength. Eisenhower appointed a McCarthy supporter to lead the Department of State's personnel program and revised the standards for dismissing government employees. Proof of disloyalty was no longer required; suspicion was sufficient. During the Eisenhower administration's first year, 2,200 government employees were fired as "security risks," but few were actually charged with disloyalty.

The witch-hunt fever infected U.S. society as a whole. Libraries threw out books considered controversial. Actors, directors, artists, intellectuals, and others were "blacklisted," making it all but impossible to find work. Some high schools even required students to sign loyalty oaths before receiving their diplomas.

olutionary forces seized Hanoi, the capital city, and declared the independent Democratic Republic of Vietnam. France, however, refused to recognize the new country. Attempting to hold on to the old colony, France became embroiled in another war.

The Soviet Union and China eventually backed Ho Chi Minh, and the United States sided with France. By 1952, 90,000 French troops had been killed, wounded, or captured. By 1954, the United States was financing about 75 percent of the struggle's costs. With casualties and costs mounting, the French and Ho Chi

Bombing in Vietnam

The Birth of the United Nations

When the League of Nations failed to prevent World War II, it folded. To many international leaders, it was obvious that another organization was needed to fill the vacuum. In late 1944, representatives from China, the Soviet Union, the United Kingdom, and the United States met at Dumbarton Oaks (in the Georgetown section of Washington, D.C.) to work out the principles for the new organization. The next year, representatives from fifty countries met in San Francisco at the United Nations Conference on International Relations.

The United Nations officially came into existence on October 24, 1945, when China, France, the Soviet Union, the United Kingdom, and the United States, along with other Member States, ratified the charter.

*An **insurgency** is a rebellion or uprising against a government.*

***Exiles** are people who have been forced to leave their country, often for political reasons.*

Sites of Soviet missiles in Cuba in 1962

Minh's government held peace talks in Geneva, Switzerland. No treaty was signed, but a series of cease-fires was established. The French would withdraw to the south and the forces of the Democratic Republic of Vietnam to the north. Within two years, elections would be held under international supervision.

Many people in South Vietnam, however, wanted to reunite with Ho Chi Minh and the Democratic Republic of Vietnam. In fact, it was estimated that in an election, Ho Chi Minh would receive 80 percent of the vote. With things looking bad for its side, South Vietnam refused to hold the elections. An **insurgency** led by the National Liberation Front (NLF), also known as the Vietcong, soon developed in the south. The United States responded by sending military advisers to South Vietnam, while simultaneously pressuring the South Vietnamese gov-

58

ernment to make reforms that would improve its popularity with their people. By 1962, more than 9,000 U.S. military advisers had been committed to the area.

THE "COMMUNIST THREAT" SPREADS

As the United States began getting bogged down in Vietnam, Americans grew concerned with another "communist threat" much closer to home. On the island of Cuba, just 93 miles (150 km) from Florida's shores, the revolutionary leader Fidel Castro had swept into power. As Castro purged the government and military of its previous leaders, many Cubans fled to the United States. With the help of the CIA and the approval of first President Eisenhower and then President Kennedy, some of these *exiles* planned an invasion to re-take Cuba. The force was small, approximately 1,400 men, but

the United States believed that once the invasion was under way it would trigger a popular uprising among the Cuban people, who would then throw off their "oppressive communist" leader.

The exiles' landing at the Bay of Pigs on April 17, 1961, was a complete fiasco. More than one hundred members of the invasion force were killed, and the rest were captured. Worse, there wasn't even a hint of a popular uprising. If anything, it seemed Castro was more popular than ever on the island. In response to the U.S. aggression, Castro officially embraced communism (something he had not previously done) and sought economic and military assistance from the Soviet Union. The entire situation was a disaster for the U.S. government.

The following year, an even bigger crisis faced Kennedy in Cuba when

President Eisenhower and President-elect Kennedy

President Johnson

the Soviet Union began building launch pads for missiles there. That meant the possibility of Soviet nuclear weapons within launching distance of American shores. Some of Kennedy's advisers favored immediate air strikes against the sites, but Kennedy feared this would lead to heavy Soviet retaliation; he understood the need for caution and diplomacy. Instead, he authorized a blockade of Cuba and demanded the installations be dismantled. On October 22, 1962, Kennedy went on national television to inform the American people of the situation, and for several days the world was as close as it has ever been to nuclear war. By October 28, however, Kennedy and Nikita Khrushchev, the leader of the Soviet Union, reached an agreement. The United States pledged no further attempts to topple Castro and promised to remove missiles from Turkey, within striking distance of the Soviet Union. The Soviets, in return, would dismantle the missile bases in Cuba. With that, the Cuban missile crisis was over.

The United States may have sidestepped war with Cuba and the Soviet Union, but back in Vietnam they were more embroiled than ever. In August 1964, North Vietnamese torpedo boats chased and attacked a U.S. destroyer in the Gulf of Tonkin. President Lyndon B. Johnson (who had succeeded to the presidency after Kennedy's assassination) sought and was granted a congressional resolution authorizing him to use force in the defense of American forces. The administration viewed the Gulf of Tonkin Resolution (as it was called) as a declaration of war.

By 1965, the Americans had effectively taken over the war against the Vietcong and North Vietnamese. The years rolled by, and the death toll steadily mounted with few clear victories for either side. Then in January 1968, the North Vietnamese launched the Tet Offensive. On Tet, the Vietnamese New Year, 80,000 North Vietnamese and Vietcong attacked military bases, cities, and towns across South Vietnam. Although it did not accomplish the complete overthrow of the South Vietnamese government as it had intended, the offensive caught American troops completely by surprise and demonstrated the ability and determination of the North Vietnamese and Vietcong forces. It became clear that while American power could keep the South Vietnamese government in

Anti-Vietnam War demonstration in 1967

New Frontier

President John F. Kennedy was elected in 1960. Perhaps as important as Kennedy's diplomacy was his idealistic rhetoric. He urged Americans, "Ask not what your country can do for you. Ask what you can do for your country." After nearly two decades mired in war and fear, the American public needed some positive thinking. Kennedy called for sacrifice and idealism from the American people and proclaimed, "I am asking each of you to be pioneers on [a] New Frontier." His administration offered greater support for civil rights. Thousands responded to his call for volunteerism and joined the newly established Peace Corps and served in foreign countries. The Kennedy administration also saw the creation of the Apollo space program, which eventually landed a man on the moon. Millions worldwide were shocked and saddened when, on November 22, 1963, his presidency was cut short by an assassin's bullet.

*Conscientious objector
status was given to otherwise
militarily qualified men who
were allowed to perform public service duties rather than
to serve in the military because of established religious
beliefs.*

*Nixon leaving the White House
after resigning*

place, it could not win the war. The cost of the war was adding up
for the American people—in bodies and in money.

The Vietnam War dominated American politics. Young men
were drafted in ever-increasing numbers. Now many were refusing
to serve, either fleeing the country or seeking *conscientious objector status*. Faced with growing opposition to the war, President
Johnson stunned his party by deciding not to seek reelection.
Republican presidential candidate Richard M. Nixon pledged he
had a plan to end the war and won election in 1968, but his plans
didn't materialize. Massive antiwar rallies were organized in the
fall of 1969, and on October 15, more than 200,000 protesters
marched on Washington in what became known as Vietnam
Moratorium Day.

Then in 1970, many Americans felt that President Nixon was expanding the Vietnam conflict when U.S. forces invaded Cambodia
to support a pro-American government. Protests erupted on college campuses across the country. On May 4, 1970, at Kent State
University in Ohio, National Guardsmen fired on a crowd of protesters, killing four and wounding nine others. In the outcry that
followed, the Senate voted to repeal the Gulf of Tonkin Resolution
and cut off further funding for troops in Cambodia.

Despite so much antiwar sentiment in the country and the
pending failure in Vietnam, the conflict dragged on for nearly five
more years. Finally, in 1975, President Gerald Ford (who assumed
office when Nixon resigned) announced that the United States was
"finished" with Vietnam. Shortly afterward, the final American
forces pulled out as Saigon, the South Vietnamese capital, fell to
the North Vietnamese army.

Watergate and Nixon's Impeachment

Despite great antiwar sentiment, in November 1972, President Nixon was reelected by a landslide. Ironically, he had not been confident of reelection. Not content with legal election tactics, Nixon's re-election committee had engaged in "dirty tricks" against his perceived foes and even broke into the Democratic National Committee Headquarters in the Watergate Hotel in Washington, D.C. This incident became known simply as Watergate.

After the election, Carl Bernstein and Bob Woodward, investigative journalists at the *Washington Post*, uncovered evidence of these crimes. In 1973, a Senate committee began its own investigation into the Watergate affair and held televised hearings that revealed the depths of Nixon's misconduct. Rather than be impeached by the U.S. Congress, President Nixon went on national television August 9, 1974, and told the American public that he would resign, effective the next day. As he climbed into the helicopter that would lift him from the White House lawn for the final time, he waved the victory sign he had made famous.

American Indians began standing up for their rights in the 1960s and '70s.

*Something that is **raucous** is unpleasantly loud.*

***Conformity** means going along with the majority.*

***Taboo** behaviors are ones forbidden or considered unacceptable by a certain group or society.*

TIMES THEY ARE A-CHANGING

For Americans, the 1950s, '60s, and '70s were largely about international conflict and war, but there was another side to these decades. They were also times of ***raucous*** social changes. The repressive atmosphere of the postwar years triggered a backlash in American culture, especially among youth. This American "counterculture" took many forms. For example, many people expressed their "alternative" view through rock music. In the 1950s, rock music began as an outgrowth of the Blues. In the 1960s and '70s, it changed into a sometimes loud and discordant musical form that often carried messages of protest against ***conformity*** and the status quo.

Many young people angrily challenged social norms by experimenting in ***taboo*** behaviors like engaging more freely in sex or using mind-altering drugs such as marijuana and LSD. Young men grew beards and long hair. But this social experimentation wasn't just about shocking people or having fun. It was about challenging people to think differently and to respect all members of society—no matter how they looked or what they believed. The right to "freedom" is often cited as a basic American value. Many people saw the protests and behaviors of the 1960s and '70s as un-American, but they were really about protecting people's freedom and were therefore quite "American" activities.

A huge civil rights movement was also under way, and it touched people from all walks of life. Many women questioned their second-class status in American society, reviving a ***feminist*** movement that had been virtually inactive since women won their voting rights. Ethnic minorities like African Americans, American Indians, and Latinos, and social minorities like gays and lesbians organized and clamored to have their rights respected by society. While American foreign policy claimed to be advancing freedom abroad, the civil rights movement demonstrated that many Americans still needed their basic human rights and freedoms granted at home.

*A **feminist** is someone who believes that women should have equality with and the same opportunities as men.*

Martin Luther King Jr. giving one of his memorable speeches

Martin Luther King Jr. was one of the most significant civil rights leaders of the 1950s and '60s. He led thousands on nonviolent campaigns for equal rights and social justice and was arrested thirty times for these activities. In 1963, King organized a march on Washington, D.C., in which he made what became his most famous speech. In that speech he declared, "I have a dream that one day this nation will rise up and live out the true meaning of its creed: 'We hold these truths to be self-evident: that all men are created equal . . . I have a dream today." In 1964, his activism earned him the Nobel Prize for Peace. Martin Luther King Jr. was assassinated in Memphis, Tennessee, on April 4, 1968.

Ronald Reagan, former leader of the American super-power

Five
THE LAST SUPER POWER STANDING

Increased cultural awareness and the civil rights movement may have been positive hall-marks of the 1970s, but the United States endured great difficulties in this era as well. America's attention had long focused on communism and Vietnam, but conflicts else-where in the world, particularly in the Middle East, were having growing affects on the United States.

In 1973, the Jewish state of Israel and the Arab states of Egypt and Syria went to war. Soon after, oil-producing Arab nations refused to sell oil to countries that supported Israel, namely the United States and its Western European allies. The oil *embargo* sent the world into an energy crisis, and the United States, the world's largest energy consumer, was the hardest hit. Fuel shortages, high prices, and long lines at the pump were common signs of the time, and the entire economy suffered under the strain.

The hard economic times continued into the 1980s. In 1980, Ronald Reagan defeated incumbent President Jimmy Carter. Reagan instituted tax cuts and hikes in defense program spending, but by 1982, the United States had entered the worst recession

*An **embargo** is a government restriction on commerce.*

The Iran–Contra Affair

Despite his popularity, the Reagan administration was far from scandal free. The biggest scandal of the Reagan years was the Iran–Contra Affair. From 1980 through 1988, Iran and Iraq were at war. Iran wanted to purchase weapons from the United States, but UN sanctions and congressional rulings forbid such sales. The Reagan administration moved ahead with arms deals anyway, partly because they thought the sales might encourage a group of terrorists in Lebanon to release American hostages (the terrorist group was sympathetic to Iran).

The illegal activities didn't end in Iran. Lieutenant Colonel Oliver North of the National Security Council funneled much of the arms-sales money to the Contras in Nicaragua. The Contras were a guerrilla group fighting to overthrow Nicaragua's Sandinista government. The Sandinistas were popular with the majority of Nicaraguans, but the Reagan administration viewed them as dangerous communists. In 1982 and 1984, Congress had denied the Reagan administration permission to finance or otherwise assist the Contras. When the arms deals and financial assistance were discovered, many members of the administration were discredited, forced to resign, fired, or even charged with crimes. How much Reagan personally knew and approved of the operation, however, was never determined.

since the Great Depression. Unemployment was rampant, and budget deficits were skyrocketing. But many big businesses and wealthy individuals flourished under Reagan's policies. Furthermore, Reagan's personality made him extremely popular with many Americans and with many people around the world.

While a struggling economy was one symbol of the 1980s, another was the weakening of the Soviet Union. Few may have realized it at the time, but the Cold War was coming to an end. Many people credit President Reagan with ending the Cold War, but to a great extent it was the Soviet Union's internal problems that assured its eventual downfall. For decades the Soviet Communist Party ruled with an iron fist. The government relied on fear, oppression, persecution, and military might to maintain power over Eastern Europe. After years of oppression, the majority of Eastern Europeans wanted change. In 1985, Mikhail Gorbachev took over as the Communist Party leader, and change was on the horizon.

THE COLD WAR "THAWS"

Mikhail Gorbachev acknowledged that the communist system was not managing the Soviet Union's economy well. While Western, democratic, capitalist economies had grown and developed innovative service sectors, the communist Soviet Union seemed locked in a rusting, antiquated, industrial economy. In an effort to make the Soviet Union more democratic, to encourage economic growth, and to establish friendlier relations with the West, Gorbachev introduced new policies called *perestroika* (restructuring) and *glasnost* (openness). He soon learned, however, that he was tampering with floodgates that, once opened, could never be closed. The whole communist system came crashing down.

Mikhail Gorbachev

Near the end of his presidency, Reagan encouraged Gorbachev to tear down the Berlin Wall, a structure built after World War II to separate Soviet-controlled East Germany from Allied-controlled West Germany. Over the years, the Wall had become perhaps the most potent physical symbol of the Cold War and the divisions between the Western and Soviet worlds. As life improved in the West and conditions worsened in the East, thousands of East Germans tried to breach the wall and were killed in the attempt. Gorbachev did not heed

George H. W. Bush

The former Soviet Union

*A **coup** is a sudden overthrow of a government, often extremely violent and done by the military.*

Map of the Soviet Union

Reagan's call, but it was not long before East Germany did. At the end of 1989, East German border guards began tearing down the Berlin Wall. Gorbachev knew that the situation was beyond the Soviet Union's ability to control and did nothing to halt the insurrection. It was a symbolic end to the Cold War.

Gorbachev's openness to the West and willingness to accept change did not make him popular with the hard-line members of his party. Fearing the total breakup of the Soviet Union, the Communist Party devised a plan to overthrow Gorbachev. It placed the Gorbachev family under house arrest, and on August 19, 1991, tanks rolled into Moscow. A **coup** had begun.

70

The Russian people, however, weren't about to cower at the hands of the Communist Party any longer. Boris Yeltsin, former mayor of Moscow, braved the snipers stationed around the square, climbed aboard one of the tanks, and called on the Russian people to resist the coup and embrace democracy. Dramatically, some of the tanks turned around to protect Gorbachev, the very person they'd been ordered to overthrow. The coup failed. Gorbachev resigned and disbanded the Communist Party. Within months, the Soviet Union dissolved, giving most Eastern European countries their independence. The super power had fallen, and the Cold War was over.

Since the Soviet Union's collapse, the United States has been the undisputed super power of the world. During and after the Cold War, the United States amassed economic and military might many times that of any other nation. This power, however, has put the United States in difficult positions, and in recent decades Americans have questioned how the power should be used. Should the United States use its might to further its own economic interests around the world? Should the U.S. military act as a "world police force"? Should the United States intervene in foreign conflicts that

President Bush in a Gulf War briefing with General Colin Powell

threaten human rights? There are no clear answers to these questions, but many times during the last two decades, the United States has been involved in each of these activities and more.

NEW CONFLICTS

While the Cold War was thawing in the early 1990s, other conflicts were just heating up. In the Middle East, Iraq invaded its oil-rich neighbor, Kuwait. U.S. President George H. W. Bush went to the United Nations seeking support to oust the Iraqi troops. Though tight economic sanctions were imposed on Iraq, Iraqi leader

Department of the Army artwork from the Gulf War

Saddam Hussein would not remove his troops from Kuwait.

After a last-minute peace mission failed, Operation Desert Storm began on January 16, 1991, with a massive attack on Iraq and Iraqi positions in Kuwait. For the next forty-two days, the United States revealed a powerful arsenal of high-tech "smart" weapons that used advanced guidance systems. When U.S. troops and their allies finally attacked Iraqi positions at the end of February, the Iraqis were beaten within four days. The short war cost the lives of 184 Americans, but an estimated 100,000 Iraqi soldiers and civilians died.

The victory over Iraq boosted morale among Americans and sent President Bush's approval ratings soaring. His popularity, however, would not withstand the challenges at home, where economic recession once again reared its head. After a campaign promise in which he famously stated, "Read my lips. No new taxes," President Bush was forced to raise taxes to deal with a swelling budget deficit. In 1992, Democratic candidate Bill Clinton pledged to "put people first," criticizing the "trickle-down" economics of Republicans, which seemed to favor corporate interests and wealthy Americans. Clinton had great personal charisma and promised to

Department of the Army artwork from the Gulf War

be a centrist—someone who would work with people from both sides of the political spectrum. He captured the White House in a contest that drew the highest voter turnout since 1972.

PROSPERITY IN THE NINETIES

Clinton's domestic aims were ambitious, and the time seemed right to address social problems that were not a priority for the previous Republican administrations. For example, at the time, 45 million Americans had no health insurance. On taking office, Clinton attempted a complete reform of the nation's health-care system. The plan, however, provoked organized opposition from insurance companies and some health-care providers. After six months of lobbying and hearings, the Clinton administration acknowledged defeat, and health-care reform was abandoned.

The defeat of health-care reform and opposition to other Clinton initiatives energized conservative Republicans, who regained control of the U.S. House of Representatives in 1994. Declaring a "Contract with America," these Republicans pledged to hold the line on spending, even to the point of disrupting government functions. The voters, however, reacted negatively to Republican **brinkmanship**, and public approval ratings for Congress dipped, while the President's remained high. He was overwhelmingly reelected in 1996.

Clinton had run on economic issues in 1992, and by 1996 the administration could point to

President William Jefferson Clinton

74

booming economic indicators. The financial markets also responded to improved budgeting in Washington; in 1997 the federal government produced a balanced budget for the following year, the first time this had happened in almost thirty years.

At the same time, the computer revolution permeated every aspect of American life. The stock market soared, largely on the strength of Internet-based companies. Trade agreements reached by the Clinton administration also boosted economic activity, although critics charged that such agreements eliminated domestic jobs.

Clinton's domestic policies weren't the only newsmakers during his *tenure*. He also had ambitious foreign policies. Within weeks of taking office, Clinton met with Russian President Yeltsin and reached an agreement to extend a moratorium on nuclear testing. He also pledged support for the newly emerging states of the former Soviet Union, which were beset by shortages and inflation as the former economic system collapsed.

The principal foreign crisis that confronted Clinton was the war in Bosnia, part of the former Republic of Yugoslavia. The strife in the mountainous country represented the largest European war since World War II, creating more than 3.5 million refugees and killing more than 100,000 people. With the European nations unable to solve the problem, the Clinton administration brokered a cease-fire in the fall of 1995 that committed U.S. troops to the region.

The U.S. economy was booming in the late 1990s, and the country was at peace, but Republicans, who controlled both branches of Congress, continued to probe Clinton, assigning a special

Brinkmanship is the practice of taking a dispute to the edge of conflict in the hope of forcing the opposition to give in on some points.

Tenure is the length of time a position is occupied.

The White House in Washington, D.C.

*If a person acts in a manner favoring a particular party or group, he is acting in a **partisan** way.*

prosecutor to investigate allegations about fund-raising. The prosecutor could not find evidence of serious fund-raising crimes, but in January 1998, he did uncover an allegation that Clinton had sexual relations with an intern in the White House. Eventually, Clinton acknowledged that he had an "inappropriate" relationship with the intern, but his personal popularity remained high. Even when the U.S. Senate began its impeachment trial of the President, polls showed that two-thirds of Americans didn't want him removed from office.

The Senate acquitted Clinton, but his standing was damaged. The 2000 presidential campaign, in which Vice President Al Gore ran against Republican George W. Bush, was bitter and close. Gore won the popular vote by more than half a million votes, but it was not enough. In the end, the election was decided in Bush's favor when the Supreme Court, along ***partisan*** lines, voted to stop a recount of Florida ballots, giving the state's disputed twenty-five

The Statue of Liberty's torch

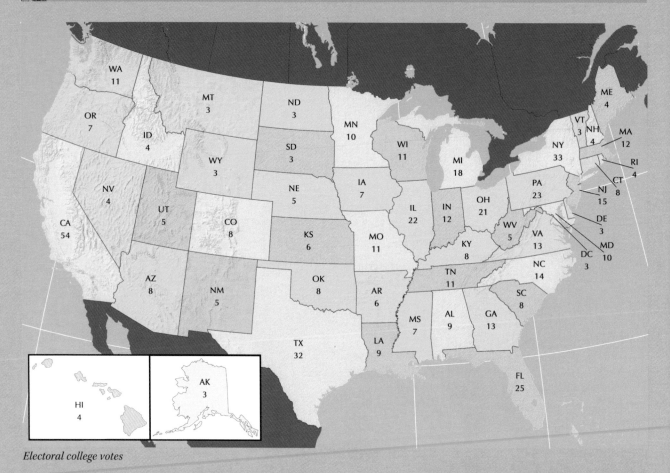

Electoral college votes

electoral votes to Bush. The country was split between those who were thrilled to have an end to the Clinton/Gore years and a return of Republican power and those who were outraged that the election had essentially been decided by unelected judges. When George Bush stepped to the inaugural podium to take his place as the first American President of the twenty-first century, he was surrounded by thousands of supporters and thousands of protestors.

The Electoral College

When the U.S. Constitution was being drafted, a serious question arose: How should the president be elected? Some people thought Congress should choose the President. This option was rejected because it could lead to corruption or upset the balance of power. Other people thought the state legislatures should elect the President, but this was also rejected because it might lead to the erosion of federal authority. Still others thought the President should be elected by popular vote. This option was rejected because of the concern that, due to the difficulty in getting information out, people would vote only for their "favorite sons."

The Electoral College was a compromise. It would allow voters to vote for electors who would then cast their votes for the candidates. The total number of a state's electors is equal to its number of senators, two, and its number of representatives, which is based on the state's population. On the Monday following the second Wednesday in December, the electors meet in their respective state capitals to cast their ballots for president and vice president. The ballots are sealed and delivered to the president of the Senate. On January 6, in front of both houses of Congress, they are opened and read.

Most of the time the candidate who gets the most popular votes also ends up with the most electoral college votes, but there have been exceptions. Four presidents have been elected although they did not receive the most popular votes: John Quincy Adams, Rutherford B. Hayes, Benjamin Hayes, and George W. Bush.

The World Trade Center

Six
AMERICA TODAY

The first months of George W. Bush's presidency passed rather quietly. The new president drew praise from many as he began work on campaign promises like a huge tax-cut package, his "Faith-Based Initiative" (a plan to make federal funding available to religious organizations for social programs), education reform, and developing a missile defense system. These measures had many critics as well, however, and President Bush was accused of proposing tax cuts that would only benefit the wealthy, ignoring separation of church and state, reverting to Cold War military philosophies, and rolling back environmental protections. He also drew criticism for spending so much of his time outside of Washington, much of it at his Texas ranch. Despite such criticisms, however, Bush's approval ratings for his first months in office remained high.

A CHANGED AMERICA, A CHANGED WORLD

When Americans awoke the morning of September 11, 2001, they had no idea that their lives were about to change forever. President George W. Bush was in Florida observing an elementary school reading class. All over America, people were going about their regular activities. Then, out of a clear blue sky, a plane crashed into one of the World Trade Center towers in New York City. Word of the shocking incident began to spread, and the media scrambled to report on what appeared to be a disastrous accident. All eyes turned to the burning tower and then watched stunned as, minutes later, a second plane veered into the other tower.

*A **fundamentalist** is one who believes in the literal interpretation of and strict adherence to a religious doctrine.*

*To do something **preemptively** means to do something before someone else can.*

***Imminent** means about to occur.*

*To **substantiate** means to confirm that something is true.*

Ground Zero in New York City

other tower.   In that moment, the realization began: these were not simply tragic accidents. Soon the confirmation began coming in. Four planes had been hijacked. The United States of America was under attack. The third plane would hit the Pentagon in Arlington, Virginia, and the fourth would crash in a field in western Pennsylvania.

The September 11 attacks shocked the world, and Americans, who had been safe and secure for so long, were shaken to the core. For many, the reality was unfathomable: someone in the world was angry enough, hated America enough, to kill thousands of innocent civilians. On September 12, President Bush spoke to the terrified American people and declared the attacks "acts of war." U.S. intelligence soon pointed the finger at a group known as al Qaeda, a ***fundamentalist*** Islamic group implicated in previous attacks on U.S. targets elsewhere in the world. The leader of the group, Osama bin Laden, was in Afghanistan, but Afghanistan's leaders, the Taliban, refused to turn over bin Laden and his comrades to the United States. On October 7, 2001, combined U.S. and British forces hit targets in Afghanistan, attempting to oust the Taliban and destroy or capture bin Laden. It seemed like the whole world sympathized with the American people and supported the American-led forces in the new "War on Terror."

After more than two months of war, the Taliban were removed from power. Bin Laden and many al Qaeda members, however, remained at large. A new leader, handpicked by the United States, was installed in Afghanistan, but his hold on power seemed tenuous at best. Outside of the capital, bandits and warlords ruled the countryside.

While the situation in Afghanistan was still chaotic, the administration was preparing for its next challenge. During President Bush's first State of the Union address on January 29, 2002, he singled out three countries as an "axis of evil": North Korea, Iran, and Iraq. Bush said these countries possessed weapons of mass destruction and represented a threat to the United States. Six months after the address, he announced a new American policy toward war. War would no longer be a last resort to be engaged in only for defense. The United States now claimed the right to **preemptively** attack any country that might pose a threat to its security. The President also identified where this new policy might take effect: Iraq. Saddam Hussein's Iraq, the administration claimed, possessed weapons of mass destruction or was seeking such weapons and intended to use them, making that nation an "**imminent** threat" to American security.

Many Americans protested both the President's new aggressive war policy and the characterization of the threat posed by Iraq. But President Bush continued to expound on the theme, and by November 2002, the United States had persuaded the UN Security Council to pass a resolution calling for enhanced weapons inspections in Iraq. The administration, however, was unwilling to allow the inspection teams the amount of time that the team leader requested. If an invasion were to occur, Pentagon officials wanted it to start in the spring, and by March, the Bush administration was calling for inspections to end. On March 17, President Bush gave Saddam Hussein two days to leave Iraq, essentially declaring war on the country. When the Iraqi leader did not leave, the United States attacked on March 19.

The reason for the war, the President said, was to prevent Iraq from using or acquiring weapons of mass destruction. No evidence of such weapons, however, had been found. Furthermore, no evidence was ever found to **substantiate** another administration claim: that there was a link between al Qaeda and Saddam Hussein. On May 1, 2003, President Bush declared that major combat in the war was over and the war won.

Despite this declaration of victory, fighting in Iraq continued as the country became increasingly unstable. With Saddam Hussein removed from power, the Iraqi military destroyed, and too few American troops to police the vast borders, anti-American groups began pouring into the war-torn country. To make matters worse, the American effort may have ousted Hussein, an undisputedly brutal dictator, but in the process it destroyed much of Iraq's *infrastructure* and killed thousands of civilians. American troops had expected to be treated as liberators, and in some early cases they were. As crime ran rampant, unemployment skyrocketed, basic services like electricity and water failed, and people continued to die, however, much of the Iraqi population lost faith in the American effort, and some even began to support the growing insurgencies. In 2004, with the conflicts between American troops and insurgents still raging, more than 80 percent of Iraqis polled said they had "no confidence" in either the United States or U.S. allies.

As the 2004 presidential election approached it was clear that America was a country divided. Democratic Senator John Kerry challenged George W. Bush for the presidency. Throughout the heated contest, critics challenged the incumbant's economic record (the economy performed poorly throughout his first term, many jobs were lost, and deficits were swelling to unprecedented proportions), war record (no weapons of mass destruction had been found in Iraq, and the U.S. military appeared mired in a conflict that had no foreseeable end), judgment (he pushed for war with Iraq while Afghanistan remained unstable and Osama bin Laden still at large), and commitment to social programs like Social Security (some analysts predicted his plans for Social Security reform would ultimately bankrupt the system). While these and numerous other charges were levied, President Bush's supporters praised his leadership after September 11 (his strong military response in Afghanistan and Iraq were viewed as decisive steps against terrorism), tax cuts (Bush theorized that

George W. Bush

cutting taxes would leave Americans with more money to spend, thereby stimulating the economy), and strong "moral character" (Bush identified himself as a born-again Christian and came out strongly against issues like gay marriage and abortion).

On November 2, 2004, the whole world watched as America voted. Many people described it as "the most important election of our lifetime," and voter turnout was the highest since 1968. When the ballots were counted, President Bush emerged with 51 percent of the popular vote compared to John Kerry's 48 percent. With enough electoral college votes to retake the White House, George W. Bush would remain as president of the strongest nation in the world for four more years.

For Americans, the early years of the twenty-first century have proven to be uncertain times. The United States may be the lone super power, but super power status cannot protect Americans from world events and their repercussions. The United States of America is by no means the world's first super power, and it almost certainly won't be its last. For now, however, the United States still holds the great responsibility of being the earth's greatest military and economic force. Debate over how to exercise this responsibility will continue to shape the American experience for years to come.

*A country's **infrastructure** is its public services and facilities, such as power and water supplies, public transportation, and roads, that are required for economic activity.*

Will 9/11's legacy be one of war—or peace?

November 11, 1918, 11:00 A.M. The German government signs an armistice, effectively ending World War I.

October 29, 1929 "Black Tuesday." The stock market collapses, signaling the beginning of the Great Depression.

1914 World War I begins.

1920 Women are given the right to vote.

1933 Adolf Hitler is appointe chancellor of Germany; he becomes president in 1934.

1917 The United States enters World War I.

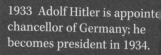

June 16, 1940 Paris falls.

December 7, 1941 Japanese planes attack Pearl Harbor, Hawaii. The United States enters World War II the next day.

1935 The Social Security Act is signed.

May 1940 Winston Churchill becomes the Prime Minister of Great Britain.

June 6, 1944 Allied forces storm the beaches at Normandy in the D-Day invasion.

September 1939 German troops invade Poland, and World War II begins.

87

May 7, 1945 Germany surrenders.

August 8, 1945 The United States drops an atomic bomb on Nagasaki, Japan, effectively ending conflict in the Pacific theater.

June 27, 1953 An armistice is signed with Korea.

June 25, 1950 North Korea invades South Korea, and President Truman commits U.S. troops to the conflict.

April 17, 1961 The Bay of Pigs invasion of Cuba fails miserably.

August 5, 1945 The United States drops an atomic bomb on Hiroshima, Japan.

1975 Saigon, capital of South Vietnam, falls to the North Vietnamese, the first U.S. war defeat.

January 16, 1991 Operation Desert Storm begins.

October 1962 The Cuban missile crisis, a standoff between the United States and the Soviet Union, occurs.

1989 The Berlin Wall is dismantled.

1963 Martin Luther King Jr. gives his famous "I have a dream . . ." speech.

September 11, 2001 Al Qaeda attacks the United States.

FURTHER READING

Blank, Carla. *Rediscovering America: The Making of Multicultural America, 1900–2000*. New York Three Rivers Press, 2003.

Carroll, Peter N. and David A. Horowitz. *On the Edge: The United States since 1945*. Belmont, Calif Wadsworth/Thompson Learning, 2002.

Crockatt, Richard. *The Fifty Years War: The United States and the Soviet Union in World Politic 1941–1991*. New York: Routledge, 1995.

Heale, M. J. *Twentieth-Century America: Politics and Power in the United States 1900–2000*. London Hodder Headline Group, 2004.

Moss, George Donelson. *America in the Twentieth Century*. Upper Saddle River, N.J.: Prentice-Hall 2004.

Payne, Stanley G. *A History of Fascism, 1914–1945*. Madison: University of Wisconsin Press, 1995.

Polenberg, Richard D. *The Era of Franklin D. Roosevelt 1933–1945*. Boston: Bedford/St. Martin's, 2000

Schultz, Bud and Ruth Schultz. *It Did Happen Here: Recollection of Political Repression in America* Berkeley: University of California Press, 1989.

Whitfield, Stephen J., ed. *A Companion to 20th-Century America*. Oxford: Blackwell, 2004.

FOR MORE INFORMATION

The Carnegie Endowment for International
Peace's Foreign Policy Web site
www.foreignpolicy.com

CIA World Factbook
www.cia.gov/cia/publications/factbook

Cold War History
www.coldwar.org

"The Globalist": A daily online magazine about
global economy, politics, and culture.
www.theglobalist.com

Information about American Imperialism
www.fordham.edu/halsall/mod/
modsbook34.html

Information about globalization
www.globalization.com

The Nuclear Weapon Archive
nuclearweaponarchive.org

The U.S. State Department
www.state.gov

World War II resources
www.ibiblio.org/pha

INDEX

Agricultural Adjustment Act 34
al Qaeda 82, 83
American internment camps 48
armistice, World War I 13
atomic bombs 49, 51
automobile 25

Bin Laden, Osama 82
"Black Tuesday" 29
Bonus Marchers 30, 31
Bureau of Investigation 22
Bush, George H. W. 71, 73
Bush, George W. 76, 78, 81, 82, 83, 84–85

Carter, Jimmy 67
Churchill, Winston 43
civil rights movement 64–65
Civilian Conservation Corps 33–34
Clinton, Bill 73–76
Cold War 51, 68, 69, 71
consumerism 24, 28
Cuba 59–60

Dust Bowl, the 32

Eisenhower, Dwight D. 56
electoral college 79
electricity, growth in use of 24–25

Emergency Relief Appropriation Act (ERA) 36
Espionage Act (1918) 20–21

Federal Deposit Insurance Corporation 35
Federal Reserve, the 29
fireside chats 36
Ford River Rouge Plant 31
Ford, Gerald 64
Ford, Henry 25

Gorbachev, Mikhail 69–71
Gore, Al 76
Great Depression, the 27–37, 43–44

Harlem Renaissance, the 25
Hitler, Adolf 37–39, 40, 41
Holocaust, the 38
Hoover, Herbert 27, 30, 31, 32
Hoover, J. Edgar 22

Industrial Workers of the World (IWW; Wobblies)
    19–20
Iraq 71, 73, 83–84

"Jazz Age" 24
Johnson, Lyndon B. 61

Kennedy, John F. 59, 60, 61
Kerry, John 84–85
King, Martin Luther, Jr. 65
Korean conflict 54–55
Ku Klux Klan (KKK) 22–23

League of Nations 16–17, 19, 57
Long, Huey 35

Marshall Plan, the 53
McCarthy Era 56
Middle East 67

National Industrial Recovery Act (NIRA) 34
National Labor Relations Board 37
National Recovery Act (NRA) 34, 36
Nationalist Socialist Workers Party (Nazi) 37–39
New Deal, the 31, 33
New York Stock Exchange 29
Nixon, Richard M. 62, 63

Pearl Harbor, Japanese attack on 44–45
presidential election 2000 76, 78
Progressive movement 19
Public Works Administration 34–35

radio, growth in popularity of 24
Reagan, Ronald 67, 68, 69–70
Red Scare 21–22
Roaring Twenties, the 23
Roosevelt, Eleanor 34
Roosevelt, Franklin D. 31–33, 36, 44
Rural Electrification Administration 37

Sacco, Nicola 22
September 11, 2001 81–82
Social Security Act 37

Soviet Union 51, 57, 60, 68–71
stock market 28–29, 75
super power, definition of 9

"talkies" 24
Treaty of Versailles 17, 19
Truman Doctrine, the 53
Truman, Harry S. 49, 53, 56

U.S. rise to super power status 9–19
United Nations 55, 57, 71, 83

Vanzetti, Bartolomeo 22
Vietnam War 56–64
vote, women win 24

Watergate 63
Wilson, Edith 18
Wilson, Woodrow 13–14, 16, 17–19
Works Progress Administration (WPA) 36–37
World War I, Allied forces in 10, 13, 14
World War I, Central Powers in 10, 13, 14
World War I, German offensive 13
World War I, U.S. involvement in 10–14, 16–19
World War II, Germany and 37–39, 40, 41, 43, 46, 47–49
World War II, Great Britain and 40, 41, 43
World War II, Japan and 40–41, 44–46, 49
World War II, Spain and 40
World War II, United States and 43–49
World War II, women in the workforce during 47

BIOGRAPHIES

AUTHOR

Eric Schwartz is a journalist living in Binghamton, New York. He received his bachelor's degree in Russian and journalism from Michigan State University and his master's degree in international relations from Syracuse University.

SERIES CONSULTANT

Dr. Jack N. Rakove is a professor of history and American studies at Stanford University, where he is director of American studies. The winner of the 1997 Pulitzer Prize in history, Dr. Rakove is the author of *The Unfinished Election of 2000, Constitutional Culture and Democratic Rule,* and *James Madison and the Creation of the American Republic.* He is also the president of the Society for the History of the Early American Republic.

PICTURE CREDITS